MASTER THIS!

Fishing

Martin Ford

WAYLAND

Published in 2013 by Wayland

Copyright © Wayland 2013

Hachette Children's Books
338 Euston Road
London NW1 3BH

Wayland Australia
Level 17/207 Kent Street
Sydney NSW 2000

Senior Editor for Wayland: Claire Shanahan
Produced by Tall Tree Ltd
Editor, Tall Tree: Jon Richards
Designer: Jonathan Vipond
Artwork: The Apple Agency

British Library Cataloguing in Publication Data
Ford, Martin.
    Fishing. -- (Master this)
    1. Fishing--Juvenile literature.
    I. Title II. Series
    799.1-dc22

ISBN: 978 0 7502 7190 5

Printed in China

Wayland is a division of Hachette Children's Books,
an Hachette UK company.

www.hachette.co.uk

Picture credits
All photos supplied by Martin Ford and Matthew
Quibell, except:
t-top, b-bottom, l-left, r-right, c-centre
cover main Dreamstime.com/Jason Kasumovic, 2
Dreamstime.com/Dohnal, 6 Dreamstime.com/Andreas
Gradin, 23tl Dreamstime.com/Dohnal, 23tc Dreamstime.
com/Vadkoz, 23ml Dreamstime.com/Sonya_m, 29b
istockphoto.com/Bob Ingelhart

The website addresses (URLs) included in this book were
valid at the time of going to press. However, because of
the nature of the Internet, it is possible that some
addresses may have changed, or sites may have changed
or closed down since publication. While the author and
publisher regret any inconvenience this may cause to
readers, no responsibility for any such changes can be
accepted by either the author or the publisher.

Disclaimer
In preparation of this book, all due care has been
exercised with regard to the advice, activities and
techniques depicted. The publishers regret that they can
accept no liability for any loss or injury sustained. When
learning a new sport it is important to get expert tuition
and to follow a manufacturer's instructions.

Contents

The world of fishing

Millions of people around the world take part in fishing, or angling. It is an exciting and relaxing sport that anyone can do, regardless of age or fitness, and it brings the angler closer to the world of nature.

Fishing over the years

Thousands of years ago, people fished using simple hooks carved from animal bones. But over the centuries, angling equipment and techniques have improved dramatically. Whether fishing for pleasure or competing in a fishing match, today's angler has a wealth of tactics and kit to choose from.

Fishing law

In most countries a **rod licence** or permit is required by law. In the United Kingdom (UK), all anglers over the age of 12 must show one. The money collected from these licences is often used to clean up rivers and ponds that have become polluted.

Fishing competitions, like the one shown here, can take place over several days, with anglers sleeping on the riverbank.

Top tip

Fishing is a sport that takes lots of patience – catching a fish can take many hours. However, you should use this time to think about alternative tactics you can use to catch fish.

Types of fishing

There are three main types of fishing: coarse fishing, game fishing and sea fishing. Coarse fishing involves fishing in lakes, ponds and rivers for all **species** of freshwater fish except salmon and trout. These two species are fished with game fishing methods, which include using a fly (see page 29). Both coarse fishing and game fishing vary slightly depending on where you are in the world. In the United States of America (USA), for example, most angling takes place in the Great Lakes, where the main species fished for is freshwater bass. Sea fishing involves fishing in saltwater, either out at sea from a boat or from the shore.

A carp is one of the largest freshwater fish and is difficult to catch. This young angler's long wait at the riverbank has paid off.

Rods, reels and poles

The equipment used by anglers is called **tackle**. There is an enormous range of tackle to choose from, including hooks, weights and nets. The most important pieces of tackle are a rod and reel or a **whip** or pole. Which one you use depends on the type of fishing you do.

Poles, whips and rods

Most beginners to freshwater fishing start out with a short pole or whip. Poles and whips usually have the fishing line tied directly to the tip and a float (see page 8) tied to the line above the baited hook. As the species being fished are usually small, they can be pulled straight out of the water once hooked, rather than wound in using a reel. As you progress, you may use a long pole, which is made up of individual sections (see pages 12–13). Alternatively, you may buy a rod with a reel if you wish to do another type of fishing, such as ledger fishing (see pages 20–21).

This fishing rod is fitted with a reel, around which the line is wound. The angler winds in the reel using the arms on its side to pull in a fish once it is caught.

rod

handle

fishing line

fishing reel

Types of fishing line

Fishing lines are graded in terms of their breaking strain – the amount of force needed to make them break. This force is measured in pounds. Lighter breaking strain lines of 2–3 pounds are used for smaller fish, while heavier lines of 5 pounds or more are used to fish for larger species.

Fishing reels

There are several types of fishing reel, each suitable for a different type of angling. The fixed spool reel is the most common type as it is suitable for all kinds of fishing, from coarse to sea. The centrepin reel is a drum-shaped reel and is

fixed spool reel

used in rivers where the force of the river pulls the reel backwards, slowly letting the float travel downstream. The multiplier reel is another drum-shaped reel, but is operated rather like the winch on a crane. It is used by sea anglers for both boat and shore fishing.

centrepin reel

multiplier reel

Loading line onto a reel

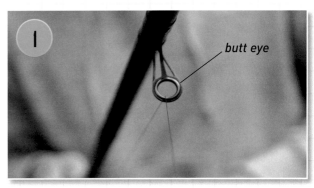

1

butt eye

Take the end of the line from the storage spool and pass it down through the butt eye of the rod before connecting it to the reel with a secure knot (see page 9).

2

Place the storage spool with the line on it into a bucket of warm water. This will help the spool to unwind smoothly. To stop the spool falling over, place a weight on top of it.

3

Start to wind the handle of the reel. This will pull the line from the storage spool to the reel spool.

Terminal tackle

Terminal tackle includes all the smaller items that are used to catch fish, including floats, hooks, feeders and split shot. The type of terminal tackle an angler uses depends on the method of fishing.

Floats, shot and weights

Floats are used to show when a fish has bitten the hook. When you get a bite, the float is dragged under the surface, disappearing from view. Floats are either made from plastic or light, **buoyant** wood, such as **balsa** wood, and come in a variety of different shapes and sizes.

Floats are weighed down in the water using small weights called split shot. Ledger weights are larger weights that are used to hold **bait** on the bottom of the lake or river (see pages 20–21). Both split shot and ledger weights are usually made from **non-toxic** material so that they do not harm wildlife.

split shot

Split shot are small, ball-shaped weights with a slit running through the middle. The fishing line is run through this slit and the balls are squeezed or pinched together so that they grip the line.

*Different shapes of fishing float suit different types of fishing. For example, waggler floats are long and slim and are used on **stillwater**. River floats have most of their body mass at the top of the float to help them float in running water.*

river floats

waggler floats

Other tackle

A hook is necessary to catch a fish when it bites on the bait (see pages 10–11). Swimfeeders (see page 21) are used to introduce loose offerings or groundbait around the hook to attract fish to the area.

hook

A disgorger is used to remove the hook from the mouth of the fish once it has been caught. Once you have caught a fish, it should be brought on land using a **landing net** and then transferred into a keepnet (see pages 26–27).

disgorger

Useful knots

The water knot
The water knot is used to join two lines together.

1

Make a loose knot in the end of one line. Feed the second line through the knot to form a loop.

2

Pass the second line back through the knot four or five times. Make sure that you wet the lines with water or saliva. This will stop friction burn on the line.

3

Pull the two ends tight to close the knot. Now trim the ends with scissors.

The half-blood loop
The half-blood loop is used to tie weights and hooks onto the line.

1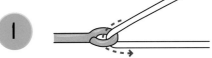

Take the end of the line and pass it through the eye of a hook.

2

Twist the end of the line around the main section of the line four times. Pass the end back through the loop closest to the hook.

3

Wet the knot with saliva or water, then pull slowly on the main line.

4

Tighten up the knot and trim off the end with scissors.

Using bait

Bait is used to attract fish to your hook. It can vary depending on the location and the species of fish you want to catch. Bait can be natural, such as maggots, or artificial, such as luncheon meat.

pellets

sweetcorn

maggots

luncheon meat

worms

casters

Keep your bait in secure containers. If storing maggots, make sure that the container has tiny air holes so that they can breathe but not escape.

Natural baits

Good natural baits include maggots, worms and slugs. Maggots are the young, or **pupae**, of the bluebottle fly. Once a maggot is grown, it will change into a chrysalis, or a 'caster', which is also a good bait. Other natural baits, such as earthworms, can be found in the garden. These are excellent baits for a number of species, especially perch.

Artificial baits

A look in any kitchen cupboard will often reveal a tin of luncheon meat or sweetcorn. Both make really good bait for larger fish such as barbel, tench and carp. Bread is also a good fishing bait. It can be used on the hook in paste form and also as something called punched bread. This is a small pellet formed by squashing the bread in a special 'bread punch'. Bread can also be used to make a groundbait.

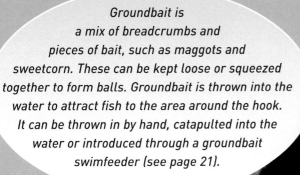

Groundbait is a mix of breadcrumbs and pieces of bait, such as maggots and sweetcorn. These can be kept loose or squeezed together to form balls. Groundbait is thrown into the water to attract fish to the area around the hook. It can be thrown in by hand, catapulted into the water or introduced through a groundbait swimfeeder (see page 21).

Hooking a maggot

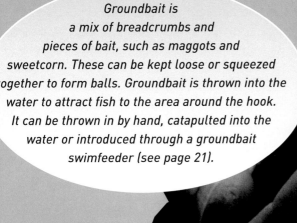

If you look very closely at the head of a maggot, you will see what appears to be two small eyes with a vent of tough skin between them.

Gently squeeze the head end of the maggot and offer up the vent to the point of the hook.

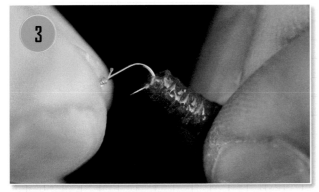

Very carefully pass the point of the hook through the vent of tough skin, making sure that you do not puncture the body of the maggot.

The maggot should hang from the hook. If using two maggots, it is better to hook them back-to-back, to stop them spinning around and hiding the hook point.

Pole fishing

Pole fishing is a method of fishing where the angler uses a long length of **carbon** pole. This has no reel, and the line with the float and hook are fitted to an internal elastic system. It is the strength of the elastic that pulls the fish into the net.

About poles

Short poles of 2–5 metres are usually called whips. A whip is fished with the line tied directly to the flexible tip. Once a fish has been hooked, it is 'whipped', or pulled, out of the water. A pole is much longer and most anglers start off with an 11-metre version, which is easier for the beginner to handle. The entire pole is made up of 11 hollow carbon sections. These sections are added and removed to put the hook into the water and to reach the correct fishing position.

Whips are suitable only for small fish species, such as roach and rudd. Here, you can see that the angler is able to raise the rod with the caught fish out of the water using one hand.

Top tip

When pole fishing, make sure you have three or four spare end sections, each with a stronger breaking strain. If you come across a large fish, attach a stronger end section and try to catch it!

Getting the hook in the water

1

Add sections onto the back of the pole, while pushing the line and hook out through the water.

2

When you have reached the required length, raise the pole to remove any slack in the line.

3

Then, lower the pole to drop the hook back down into the water and start fishing.

pole

PTFE bush

elastic

line

Pole elastic

The internal elastic system runs through the end three sections of the pole. This is a length of elastic that has been secured to the back of the third section. At the very tip of the pole there is a 'PTFE bush'. When a fish bites, the elastic is pulled out of the top of the pole. The PTFE bush is made from a special material that is self-**lubricating**. This makes sure that the elastic stretches smoothly.

Star file

TONY KIRRAGE
Sea and carp angler

Tony Kirrage has been fishing for more than 30 years. He began his career in sea angling competitions, representing the UK at international level, and has won the West African Shore Championships. In 2004 and with a switch of angling methods, Tony and partner Mick Hindson won the World Carp Classic at Lac Amance, France. He has filmed several angling DVDs and written many articles on fishing for magazines around the world.

More about pole fishing

To be a successful pole angler, there are several items of tackle that you should buy, including floats, float rubbers, line winders, olivettes, hooks and lines. You also need a seat box to sit on, as you will want to be comfortable during many hours of fishing.

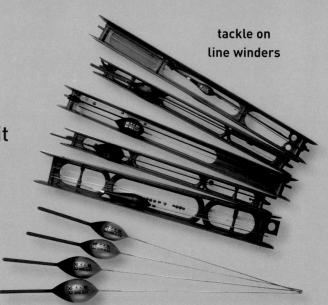

tackle on line winders

pole floats

Floats, rubbers and winders

Pole floats are made from a variety of materials, such as carbon, plastic and wood, and they come in different shapes to suit different situations. Pole float rubbers are small pieces of fine rubber tubing that have a narrow hole and are used to attach the float to the line. Winders are storage devices that the whole rig (line, weights, float and hook) can be wound around at the end of a day's fishing.

When holding a pole, lay the back end of the pole across your knee. Push one hand down on the rear of the pole to hold it steady. Put your forward hand underneath the pole, ready to lift it gently when a bite occurs.

Other pole fishing tackle

Olivettes are a type of bulk weight used with larger pole floats. They are attached to the line below the float and drag the bait down through the water. Most pole anglers tend to favour thin hooks as the presentation of the bait will appear more natural to the fish.

Ordinary line, similar to the type you would wind onto a reel, is perfectly acceptable to use as a pole fishing main line. However, many anglers prefer to use very fine lines, relying on the pole's internal elastic to take the weight once a fish is hooked. When a fish bites, pull in the pole until you are holding the top three sections. The elastic stretches as the fish pulls away and then, as the elastic springs back, the fish is pulled to the surface and into your net.

Top tip

When you have finished for the day, store your complete rig onto a line winder and mark details such as the depth from float to hook on the side. You will then have a rig ready for your next trip.

Putting an olivette onto the line

Thread two small sections of thin silicon rubber tubing onto the fishing line. The olivette has two extending pins at its ends and a groove along its middle.

Slide the pins into the silicon and run the fishing line through the central groove.

Push the silicon rubber down firmly over the olivette's pins so that the weight is held securely on the fishing line.

15

Float fishing in stillwater

When float fishing, an angler uses a rod and reel that has a float attached to the line. Float fishing allows you to fish the whole depth of the water, not just the bottom, as with ledger fishing (see pages 20–21).

Stillwater float fishing kit

In most stillwater float fishing situations you are not likely to come across large species such as carp. So a three-piece rod and a small, fixed spool reel loaded with 3-pound line (see page 6) should be fine. Floats for stillwater fishing are long and thin and are called wagglers. They are made from light materials such as plastic or balsa wood.

Top tip

Always carry a selection of different lengths of waggler float when you go stillwater fishing. The longer the float, the deeper and farther out you will be able to fish.

A young angler is float fishing in a small pond. To his side are two boxes containing a variety of baits to suit different fish.

Set-up for stillwater

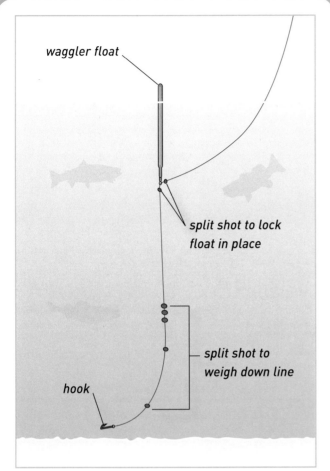

- waggler float
- split shot to lock float in place
- split shot to weigh down line
- hook

The waggler float is held in place using split shot. If you want to fish at a depth of 2 metres, use split shot to lock the float 2 metres up from the hook. Other split shot weighs the rest of the line down in the water.

This waggler float has split shot attached to its base to lock it to the line. Markings on the side show how much weight is needed to make it 'cock' (sit up in the water at the correct height).

Using a plummet

When float fishing, you need to use a plummet to find out exactly how deep the water is so you can set the float correctly. A plummet is a lead weight that must be heavier than the float. If the plummet drags the float below the surface, you have set the float too shallow, and if your float is still visible, you have it set too deep. You will need to make adjustments to the depth that the float has been set from the hook, until you arrive at the correct setting.

Plummet weights are attached to the hook to test the depth of the water.

Fishing in running water

Float fishing in running water, such as rivers and streams, requires a good level of skill because the float and bait have to move with the flow of the water. Once mastered, it is a great way to catch freshwater species such as roach, dace and chub.

Running water float fishing

For running water, you can use a similar rod and reel to stillwater float fishing. However, some anglers prefer to use a longer rod, measuring 4 or 4.5 metres. This allows more control over a float that is being 'trotted' down the river. **Trotting** is the term for allowing the float to travel at the same speed as the current, but under the control of the angler. This is done by allowing line to run off the spool of the reel, but under check.

Star file

TIM PAISLEY
Carp angler

British angler Tim Paisley won two World Carp Championships, in 2000 at Lac Fishabil, France, and in 2005 on the great St Lawrence River, USA. Both wins were with partner Steve Briggs. Tim has contributed to most of the carp fishing magazines around the world and, at the age of 70, continues to fish the international circuit.

Set-up for running water

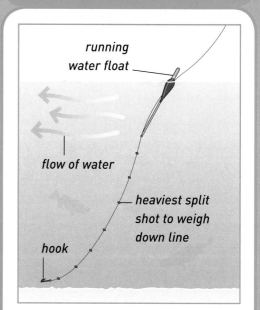

running water float

flow of water

heaviest split shot to weigh down line

hook

The line is weighted with a string of split shot, with the heaviest shot halfway between the float stem and the hook. The remaining shots, which are lighter in weight, are then spread along the length of the line. This ensures that the hook bait gets down through the flowing water.

1 This basic **cast** applies both to float or ledger fishing. Start by opening up the bale arm on the reel.

2 You will still need to trap the line with your finger to stop it from falling off the reel.

3 Take the rod behind your head as shown. Focus on where in the water you want the float to be cast.

4 Pull down on the handle of the rod and push forwards, letting go of the line as the rod passes overhead.

Floats and bait

Some river floats are quite long, so three float rubbers should be used to attach them to the line, one above the float body and two below. When fishing with this type of float, it is possible to hold the float back slightly by applying pressure to the line with your finger as it comes off the reel. This causes the hook bait to rise up off the bottom and then fall back down, drawing attention to the bait. It is also a good idea to keep plenty of free bait in the water to attract fish to the hook bait.

Floats for river fishing will have the bulk of the body at the top of the float, ensuring that they float correctly in the flow. They are made from plastic, balsa wood and **cane***. The traditional 'crow quill' float has a balsa body and a* **quill** *stem.*

19

Ledger fishing

The term 'ledger' means to fish on the bottom of a lake or river, using a weight to hold down the end tackle. It is a very simple form of fishing and can be a good tactic to use on rivers in particular.

Ledger weights keep the hook and bait on the bottom of the water. A variety of small weights will cover most situations.

Ledger tackle

Ledger rods are usually 3–3.5 metres long. Instead of using a float to show whether or not there has been a bite, they either have a screw-in attachment at the tip, or what is called a spliced-in quiver tip. The screw-in attachment is for fitting a swing-tip or flexible quiver tip. The swing-tip is a solid arm, about 20 centimetres long, with a screw thread at one end and one or two eyes at the other. When a bite occurs, the swing-tip rises.

quivertip

*This angler is using a quiver tip at the end of his rod. The quiver tip is a thin, flexible length of carbon or **fibreglass**. It is fished out to one side and under slight pressure with the line. This creates a slight curve in the quiver tip. If a bite occurs, the quiver tip bends, as shown here.*

Set-up for ledger fishing

Ledger end tackle consists of a ledger weight that is stopped by a bead. The bead rests against a swivel, a small brass barrel that stops the two ends of the line from tangling. To the other side of the swivel is a short length of 3-pound line that runs down to the hook. This line is called the hooklength and, the smaller the species you are after, the finer this hooklength line can be.

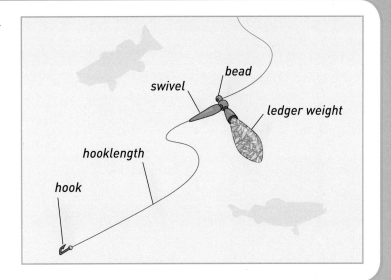

Ledger fishing tactics

A small fixed spool reel capable of holding 100 metres of 5–6 pound line (see page 6) should be adequate for most ledger fishing situations. Anglers who want to catch bream prefer to use a swimfeeder instead of a ledger weight. There are two types of swimfeeder: open-end feeders which are used in stillwater, while block-end feeders are used when river fishing.

Top tip

For ledger fishing in stillwater, use an open-end feeder packed with groundbait (see pages 10–11). For ledger fishing in running water, try a block-end feeder filled with maggots.

A cage-style open-end feeder is used in stillwater and can be plugged with groundbait. A 'method' feeder is used for larger species, such as carp. Groundbait is moulded around its wire frame.

method feeder

cage-style feeders

Stillwater fishing

As a beginner to angling, you will probably start off by fishing a pond or shallow canal, catching small roach and perch. After a while, you may want to try fishing for larger species and will naturally progress onto larger stretches of water, such as lakes and rivers.

Commercial fisheries

Commercial **fisheries** are purpose-built places that have a variety of freshwater species, such as bream, tench and carp (see page 23). Pole fishing is popular at fisheries, using small bait, such as single maggots, to catch smaller fish. Fishing with a ledger set-up or a swimfeeder packed with groundbait often brings bites from bream and tench. To catch larger species, you need to consider stronger tackle and larger bait, such as luncheon meat.

Commercial fisheries tend to be busy, especially during the summer months. Most have purpose-built fishing platforms to fish from.

tench

mirror carp

bream

Gravel pits and lakes

Lakes or flooded gravel pits are not as easy to fish as commercial fisheries. The water may contain a natural stock of fish, or it is possible that a fishing club has also stocked it. The species that can be caught are likely to be fewer but larger than those at a commercial fishery, and you will have to think hard about your approach.

At this type of fishery, most anglers would usually use a rod and reel, either with a float or ledger fishing approach. Poles can be used, but generally for smaller fish. Stronger tackle may be needed for larger bream, tench and carp, and it is likely that the water will contain weed beds and other objects you could catch your line on.

This tench has been caught at a commercial fishery. The anglers have placed an unhooking mat underneath their net. The mat is an important piece of equipment and many fisheries insist that you have one (see pages 26–27).

Top tip

Carry a variety of different baits with you when fishing in stillwater, so you are able to change your hook bait approach for the many different species you are likely to come across.

Rivers and canals

Rivers and canals offer a wealth of fishing opportunities, and they will be home to several species, some of which are not usually found in stillwaters (see page 25). Rivers and canals present very different challenges from the calmer waters found in lakes and fisheries.

(see page 25)

River fish

Different sections of a river will be home to different species of fish. The slower parts of a river will usually hold larger fish, such as bream, perch and barbel (above). Shallower sections will be home to dace, bleak, roach and chub.

Rivers

The speed and depth of a river will vary along its length, and different fishing tactics will suit different sections. Both float fishing and ledger fishing with a rod and reel are popular methods to use. Due to the flow and the larger size of the species, your tackle will need to be stronger than that used on a canal or stillwater. Baits will vary, but worms, maggots, bread flake and even luncheon meat are all worth taking.

River fishing is slightly harder than stillwater or canal fishing as the water is moving. This means that any presentation, such as a float, will need to move with the flow.

Canals tend to have a shallow area at each side with a deeper channel down through the centre. This deeper channel is called a boat track and is usually where the bigger fish are found.

Top tip

It is worth taking bread as bait to a canal. This can be fed as groundbait and also used on the hook as bread punch (see page 10) to attract all types of canal fish, especially bream and carp.

Canals

Most canals will be narrow and very shallow and they will be home to small species such as roach, bleak, perch, rudd, bream and tench, with the possibility of a few larger carp and pike. The most popular tactic on a canal is to use either a short whip or a long pole. However, the best places to fish on canals are in the canal basins. These are much deeper and wider and are usually home to larger species, such as tench and bream. Bait for canal fishing is varied, but small baits such as maggots and bread punch usually work well.

Looking after your catch

It is very important that you care for the fish you catch before you return them to the water. By doing this, you are giving other anglers a chance to catch the fish.

Keepnets

A keepnet is a netted tube used to hold fish after they are caught. Most fisheries ask that the keepnet you use is made from a fish-friendly material. They may ask you to dip your nets in a special tank of antiseptic to stop diseases spreading. Some fisheries supply their own keepnets, or ban the use of them. Others request that you bring two keepnets. One is used for sliver fish, such as roach and bream, and the other for larger carp, which can be a very lively species and might damage other fish in the net.

A landing net containing a large carp is gently lowered into a blue keepnet. You should not throw a fish into a keepnet. Instead, lean forward and gently let the fish slide from your hand or the landing net into the keepnet.

Conservation

One important matter that all anglers should really care about is conservation. You should take care of the fish you catch and the environment you fish in. Take note of any special fishing conditions and make sure that your tackle is non-toxic.

Also, look out to see if your fish has any injuries. These can be treated on the bank so that the fish stays healthy. By looking after your catch and returning it to the water unharmed, you ensure that there are plenty of fish for other anglers.

Using a disgorger

If the caught fish is quite small, try to unhook it while it is still in your landing net. Larger fish should be lowered gently onto an unhooking mat.

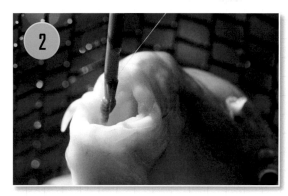

Carefully loop the disgorger around the hook inside the fish's mouth and ease it out, without damaging the fish.

Unhooking mat

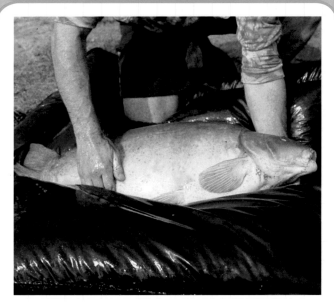

Fisheries where large carp are fished insist that anglers use a heavily padded unhooking mat. This thick mat protects a heavy fish after it has been caught.

Top tip

Some anglers carry a pair of forceps as well as a disgorger. Forceps are useful if you are pike fishing and have to deal with a mouth full of razor-sharp teeth!

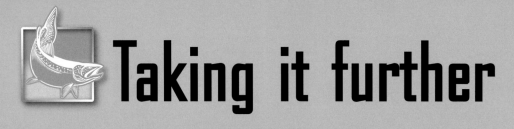

Taking it further

Once you have all the basic knowledge of float fishing, ledger fishing and pole fishing, you might decide that you want to develop one of these methods further. You might even want to dedicate your angling time to one particular species, such as carp.

Top tip

Do not be afraid to ask questions of other anglers when you are on the bank, and spend time watching instead of fishing – you will be able to apply what you learn to your own angling.

Specialist anglers need tackle that is specifically designed to catch one species of fish. This specialist carp angler is resting his rods on bite alarms he has rigged up on the riverbank.

bite alarm

Clubs

Many fishing clubs have competitive events throughout the year, and once you join a particular club you will be able to enter these matches. Most angling clubs will also offer coaching. Angling clubs and associations will have their own waters and you will be able to use these for a small joining fee. Most countries have an international match team and they compete with each other at the World Coarse Angling Championships each year.

Beyond coarse fishing

You may want to take your fishing experience even further and try out some of the other types of angling. Game fishing is a skilful form of angling and involves specialist tackle and an artificial lure called a fly. Sea fishing can take you out into the oceans, chasing large fish, such as tuna, sailfish, marlin and even sharks!

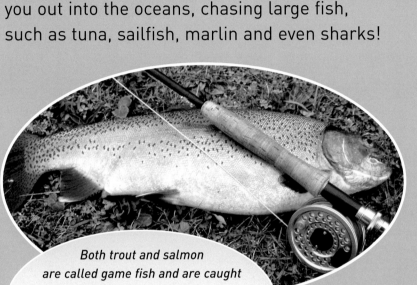

Both trout and salmon are called game fish and are caught using specialist tackle. This trout was caught using a fly rod and a fly reel, which has a special coated line on it that floats on the surface.

This sea angler has caught a large sea fish, called a mahi-mahi.

Glossary

bait something used to attract fish to the hook. Bait can be live, such as maggots, or household foods such as luncheon meat or sweetcorn.

balsa a light, quick-growing wood. Balsa wood can float on water, which makes it very good for making fishing floats.

buoyant the ability of an object to float in water. For example, fishing floats need to be buoyant so that they float at the water's surface, whereas ledger weights are not buoyant and will sink to the bottom.

cane a short stick made from a piece of bamboo. Since bamboo can float, it is sometimes used to make fishing floats.

carbon short for carbon fibre, this is a very light but strong material that is made up of tiny, microscopic fibres of carbon.

cast throwing the fishing line, with the hook, weights and float, out into the water so that it lands some distance from the bank and the angler.

fibreglass a strong but lightweight material that is made up of strands of very thin fibres of glass.

fisheries a place where fish are bred for sport or food. At fisheries for anglers, the fish are usually returned to the water.

landing net a net for lifting a fish out of the water once it has been hooked.

lubricating making something moist so that it moves more smoothly and with less friction. For example, soaking your new line in water will make it smoother when you fish with it.

pupae the young of an insect. For example, the young of flies are maggots, which are good to use as bait. When the pupae grow up, they change into a chrysalis before turning into an adult fly.

non-toxic something that is not poisonous. For example, floats and weights will be made of non-toxic material to avoid contaminating water and wildlife.

quill the feather from a bird. Quills can float on water and were used to make fishing floats before the invention of plastics.

rod licence a legal permit to fish.

stillwater water in ponds or lakes that does not flow in a current.

tackle the term used to describe the equipment used by an angler, including the rod or pole, reels, hooks, weights and floats.

species a type of living thing, such as a plant or animal. For example, carp, bream and barbel are all species of fish.

trotting allowing a float to move out with the flow of running water, such as flowing water in a stream or river.

whip a long, flexible rod used for catching light species of fish.

Fishing organisations

For the angler who wants to get into the specialist world of fishing and seeks to catch just one particular species, there are now many organisations around the world that are dedicated to this.

The Carp Society in the UK and the USA caters for the needs of the carp angler, as does the Tench Fisher's Club.

The game angler has the Salmon and Trout Association and the Fly Tyer's Guild. The sea angler has the National Federation of Sea Anglers, plus other worldwide groups.

The Angling Trust is an organisation created by the merger of several other groups. It was set up to represent anglers from all disciplines.

Further reading

There are plenty of books available for the newcomer as well as the more experienced angler.

Get Outdoors: Fishing Nick Ross (Wayland, 2008)

How To... Go Fishing and Catch Fish Gareth Purnell (Franklin Watts, 2007)

Know Your Sport: Fishing Clive Gifford (Franklin Watts, 2007)

The Little Book of Fishing Tips Michael Devenish (Absolute Press, 2007)

Websites

The Internet is a great place for information on clubs, associations, events and venues to fish at.

www.fishing.com

Links to fishing websites from around the world, including national and international organisations and tutorials.

www.fishing.net

A fishing network site with tips, reports, news and blogs submitted by anglers from around the world.

www.creativeon-line.com/tipsimages/tipspage2.html

Website aimed at kids with tips on the best techniques and equipment for the young angler.

Index